Political Quotes

Compiled by

MICHAEL ROGERS

SPHERE BOOKS LIMITED
London and Sydney

First published in Great Britain by
David & Charles (Publishers) Limited 1982
Copyright © Hearn Stephenson Publishing Limited 1982
Published by Sphere Books Ltd 1984
30–32 Gray's Inn Road, London WC1X 8JL

TRADE
MARK

Set in Baskerville

Printed and bound in Great Britain by
Cox & Wyman Ltd, Reading

Introduction

'With words we govern men,' declares a character in Disraeli's novel *Contarini Fleming*. Ridiculous, we might think, when we know how threadbare the language of politics can be, debased by the intellectual anaesthesia of euphemism, cliché, woolliness and bombast. Yet political three-card tricks still work as well as they always have, and if it is true, as the American poet, e.e. cummings, said, that 'a politician is an arse upon which everyone has sat except a man', we regularly vote for orifices rather than oracles.

In this concise anthology I have tried to concentrate on quotations which are in some way arresting in their own right, as against those statements of philosophical or historical importance expressed without colour or vivacity. Style does not always have to be lapidary, but a little gleam of wit makes for more interesting reading (although it is especially true in matters political that all that glisters is not gold) and, unlike most politicians, I have gone for brevity – aphorism over sophism.

One or two things may strike the reader. For example, the impressive amount of bitchiness embodies a passionate conviction, which gives it an integrity setting it apart from the four-square statements of an exemplary and idealistic kind. The House of Commons often promotes a style of knock-down, drag-out debate rich in jibe, put-down and send-up with honourable members baying at each other like packs of rival football supporters. On the other hand, the debates of its American counterpart seem strangely etiolated for a country which prides itself on robust directness. However, in compensation, American presidents are often wonderfully acrobatic – putting both feet in their mouth at the same time.

Happily for the anthologist there are wits as well as twits on both sides of the Atlantic, and political language and lore would be poorer without the verbal stilettoes of Churchill, Adlai Stevenson and F. E. Smith, the sledge-hammers of Lyndon Johnson or Harry Truman or the jokes of Henry Kissinger. And, luckily, no one has yet taken Philip Snowden's advice: 'It would be desirable if every government, when it comes into power, should have its old speeches burned.' Not even Richard M. Nixon managed that.

Michael Rogers

What are Politicians?

A politician is a statesman who approaches every question with an open mouth.

Adlai Stevenson

A politician is an animal who can sit on a fence and keep both ears to the ground.

H. L. Mencken

A politician is a man who understands government... A statesman is a politician who's been dead ten or fifteen years.

Harry S. Truman

A politician is an arse upon which everyone has sat except a man.

e. e. cummings, 'A Politician'

A politician is a person with whose politics you don't agree. If you agree with him, he is a statesman.

Lloyd George

When you're abroad you're a statesman; when you're at home you're just a politician.

Harold Macmillan

An ambassador is an honest man sent to lie abroad for the commonwealth.

Sir Henry Wotton, 1604

Bumptious Idiots and Born Rulers

Every bumptious idiot thinks himself a born ruler of men....

> *George Bernard Shaw,*
> The Intelligent Woman's Guide to Socialism

Every politician is emphatically a promising politician.
> *G. K. Chesterton,* The Red Moon of Meru

The most successful politician is he who says what everybody is thinking most often and in the loudest voice.

> *Theodore Roosevelt*

It is a general popular error to imagine the loudest complainers for the public to be the most anxious for its welfare.

> *Edmund Burke*

The best lack all conviction, while the worst
Are full of passionate intensity.
> *W. B. Yeats,* The Second Coming

He knows nothing and he thinks he knows everything. That points to a political career.
> *George Bernard Shaw*, Major Barbara

The men who really believe in themselves are all in lunatic asylums.

> *G. K. Chesterton*, Orthodoxy

I remain just one thing, and one thing only – and that is a clown. It places me on a far higher plane than any politician.

Charlie Chaplin

Odd things animals. All dogs look up to you. All cats look down to you. Only a pig looks at you as an equal.

Winston Churchill

I always wanted to get into politics but I was never light enough to get in the team.

Art Buchwald

We are not politicians. We made our revolution to get the politicians out.

Fidel Castro, 1961

Ah, these diplomats! What chatterboxes! There's only one way to shut them up – cut them down with machine guns! Bulganin, go and get me one!

Stalin (reported by de Gaulle)

Politicians are the same all over. They promise to build a bridge even when there's no river.

Nikita Khrushchev

Few politicians are masochists.

Harold Wilson

The graveyards are full of indispensable men.

Charles de Gaulle

A few honest men are better than numbers.

Oliver Cromwell

There is no connexion between the political ideas of our educated class and the deep places of the imagination.

Lionel Trilling, The Liberal Imagination

Shakespeare, in the familiar lines, divided great men into classes: those born great, those who achieve greatness, and those who have greatness thrust upon them. It never occurred to him to mention those who hire public relations experts and press secretaries to make themselves look great.

Daniel Boorstin, The Image

There is only one political career for which women are perfectly suited: diplomacy.

Clare Booth Luce

There are too many men in politics and not enough elsewhere.

Hermione Gingold

. . . a politician rises on the backs of his friends (that's probably all they're good for).

Richard Hughes, The Fox in the Attic

I'm not a politician and my other habits are good.

Artemus Ward, Artemus Ward His Book

The trouble with this country is that there are too many politicians who believe, with a conviction based on experience, that you can fool all the people all of the time.

Franklin P. Adams, Nods & Becks, 1944

Since a politician never believes what he says, he is surprised when others believe him.

Charles de Gaulle

If experience teaches us anything at all, it teaches us this: that a good politician, under democracy, is quite as unthinkable as an honest burglar.

H. L. Mencken

Our great democracies still tend to think that a stupid man is more likely to be honest than a clever man, and our politicians take advantage of this prejudice by pretending to be even more stupid than nature made them.

Bertrand Russell

The Art of the Possible

Politics is the art of the possible.

R. A. Butler

Politics is not the art of the possible. It consists in choosing between the disastrous and the unpalatable.
J. K. Galbraith

Being in politics is like being a football coach. You have to be smart enough to understand the game and stupid enough to think it's important.

Eugene McCarthy

I have come to the conclusion that politics are too serious to be left to the politicians.

Charles de Gaulle

Politics is the art of looking for trouble, finding it whether it exists or not, diagnosing it incorrectly and applying the wrong remedy.

Sir Ernest Benn

City government is of the people, by the rascals, for the rich.

Lincoln Steffens

It is now known that men enter local politics solely as a result of being unhappily married.
G. Northcote Parkinson, Parkinson's Law

Politics are not my concern.... They impress me as a dog's life without a dog's decencies.

> *Rudyard Kipling*, A Diversity of Creatures

Politics is perhaps the only profession for which no preparation is thought necessary.

> *R. L. Stevenson*, Familiar Studies of Men and Books

...Parliamentary democracy in this country, if not dead already, is in the latter stages of terminal sickness.

> *Cyril Smith*, MP

Politics is no exact science.

> *Otto von Bismarck*

... the systematic organization of hatreds.

> *Henry Adams* (on politics), 1907

Politics n. A strife of interests masquerading as a contest of principles.

> *Ambrose Bierce*, The Devil's Dictionary

Politics are almost as exciting as war and quite as dangerous. In war you can only be killed once, but in politics many times.

> *Winston Churchill*

Politics is war without bloodshed.

> *Mao Tse-Tung*

Politics is the diversion of trivial men who, when they succeed at it, become important in the eyes of more trivial men.

> *George Jean Nathan*

All politics are based on the indifference of the majority.

> *James Reston*

The Contrivance of Human Wisdom

Government is a contrivance of human wisdom to provide for human wants. Men have a right that these wants should be provided for by this wisdom.

Edmund Burke

Freedom is not enough.

Lyndon Johnson

Democracy means government by the uneducated, while aristocracy means government by the badly educated.

G. K. Chesterton

It has long been a grave question whether any government not too strong for the liberties of its people can be strong enough to maintain its liberties in great emergencies.

Abraham Lincoln

Despotism tempered by assassination.
Lord Reith's idea of the best form of government

Let our children grow tall – and some grow taller than others...

Margaret Thatcher

A state without the means of some change is without the means of its conservation.

Edmund Burke

To innovate is not to reform.

Edmund Burke

All reforms except a moral one will prove unavailing.

Thomas Carlyle

Democracy means government by discussion, but it is only effective if you can stop people talking.

Clement Attlee

The tree of liberty must be refreshed from time to time with the blood of patriots and tyrants. It is its natural manure.

Thomas Jefferson

Democracy is like a raft. It never sinks, but, damn it, your feet are always in the water.

Fisher Ames

If any ask me what a free government is, I answer, that for any practical purpose it is what people think so.

Edmund Burke

Liberty... must be limited in order to be possessed.

Edmund Burke

Q: Have you ever taken a serious political stand on anything?
A: Yes, for 24 hours I refused to eat grapes.

Woody Allen, Sleeper

The only good government... is a bad one in a hell of a fright.

Joyce Cary, The Horse's Mouth

Liberty doesn't make men happy; it merely makes them men.

Manuel Azana, President of the Second Republic

Diplomacy is the police in grand costume.

Napoleon Bonaparte

The art of governing exists in not letting men grow old in their jobs.

Napoleon Bonaparte

Whenever you have an efficient government you have a dictatorship.

Harry S. Truman

Everything starts as a mystique and ends as politics.

Graffito, Paris, May 1968

In order that the people may be free, it is necessary that the governed be sages and those who govern gods.

Napoleon Bonaparte

In general, the art of government consists in taking as much money as possible from the one part of the citizens to give to the other.

Voltaire

Democracy is the theory that the common people know what they want, and deserve to get it good and hard.

H. L. Mencken

Realpolitik

... there is nobody in the world who submits to anything but force.

Ernest Bevin

Necessity hath no law.

Oliver Cromwell

We had no use for the policy of the Gospels: if someone slaps you, just turn the other cheek. We had shown that anyone who slapped us on our cheek would get his head kicked off.

Nikita Khrushchev

Those republics which in times of danger cannot resort to a dictatorship will generally be ruined, when grave occasions occur.

Machiavelli

When you are skinning your customers, you should leave some skin on to grow so that you can skin them again.

Nikita Khrushchev

A lie is an abomination to the Lord and a very present help in trouble.

Adlai Stevenson

Oderint, dum metuant (Let them hate so long as they fear).

Lucius Accius, 170-*c*.85 BC

It has always been desirable to tell the truth but seldom if ever necessary to tell the whole truth.

A. J. Balfour

Only constant repetition will finally succeed in imprinting an idea on the memory of the crowd.

Adolf Hitler, Mein Kampf

The great mass of the people... will more easily fall victim to a big lie than to a small one.

Adolf Hitler, Mein Kampf

The terror is nothing but justice...

Robespierre

If we see that Germany is winning the war we ought to help Russia, and if Russia is winning we ought to help Germany, and in that way let them kill as many as possible.

Harry S. Truman

Let them put their demands in such a way that Great Britain could say she supported both sides.

Ramsay MacDonald

Nixon: A cover-up is the main ingredient.
Colson: That's the problem...
Nixon: That's where we gotta cut our losses. My losses are to be cut. The President's losses gotta be cut on the cover-up deal.

Richard Nixon to Charles Colson, 14 February 1973

I don't know much about Americanism, but it's a damn good word with which to carry an election.

Warren G. Harding

Use all the rhetoric, so long as it doesn't cost money.

Richard M. Nixon

I would rather be an opportunist and float than go to the bottom with my principles round my neck.

Stanley Baldwin

I work for a government I despise for ends I think criminal.

J. M. Keynes

Our Masters Now

Our supreme governors, the mob.

Horace Walpole

There's a lot of bleeding idiots in t' country, and they deserve some representation.

Bill Stone, MP

Your representative owes you, not his industry only, but his judgement; and he betrays instead of serving you if he sacrifices it to your opinion.

Edmund Burke

The people of the world respect a nation that can see beyond its own image.

John F. Kennedy

I tremble for my country when I reflect that God is just.
Thomas Jefferson

I'm for the common people. The only trouble is, there ain't no common people in Beverly Hills.
Will Rogers, running for mayor of Beverly Hills

I hate elections, but you have got to have them; they are medicine.

Stanley Baldwin

All men would be tyrants if they could.

Daniel Defoe

If people have to choose between freedom and sandwiches they will take sandwiches.

Lord Boyd-Orr

A Parliament elected by the universal suffrage of voters grouped according to geographical areas is about as truly representative as a bottle of Bovril is a true representative of an ox.

Eleanor Rathbone

Once the people begin to reason all is lost.

Voltaire

If any demonstrator ever lays down in front of my car, it'll be the last car he'll ever lay down in front of.

George Wallace

Voters quickly forget what a man says.

Richard M. Nixon

In those days we had a real political democracy led by a hierarchy of statesmen and not a fluid mass distracted by newspapers.

Winston Churchill, My Early Life

I must follow them; I am their leader.

Andrew Bonar Law

The General Strike has taught the working class more in four days than years of talking could have done.

Arthur Balfour

If the British public falls for this, I say it will be stark staring bonkers.

Lord Hailsham

How could a state be governed... if every individual remained free to obey or not to obey the law according to his private opinion?

Thomas Hobbes

I will not take the word of the people from a few demagogues any more than I will take the word of God from a few priests.

Charles James Fox

Many politicians... are in the habit of laying it down as a self-evident proposition that no people ought to be free till they are fit to use their freedom. The maxim is worthy of the fool... who resolves not to go into the water till he had learned to swim.

Thomas Babington Macaulay

It's a recession when your neighbour loses his job, it's a depression when you lose your own.

Harry S. Truman

Votes are to swords exactly what bank notes are to gold – the one is effective only because the other is believed to lie behind it.

F. E. Smith, Earl of Birkenhead

Many people consider the things which government does for them to be social progress, but they consider the things government does for others as socialism.

Chief Justice Earl Warren

Let the people think they govern and they will be governed.

William Penn, 1693

Governments arise either out of the people or over the people.

Thomas Paine, The Rights of Man, 1791

Your public servants serve you right; indeed often they serve you better than your apathy and indifference deserve.

Adlai Stevenson

What we call public opinion is generally public sentiment.

Benjamin Disraeli

The people like neither the true nor the simple; they like novels and charlatans.

Edmond and Jules de Goncourt

The Exercise of Power

Power tends to corrupt, and absolute power corrupts absolutely. Great men are almost always bad men.
Lord Acton

Power corrupts, but lack of power corrupts absolutely.
Adlai Stevenson

Swinton: If you treated me as you do Curzon I would quit. I cannot understand why Curzon does not resign.
Lloyd George: Oh, but he does, constantly. But there are two messengers in the Foreign Office: one has a club foot, he comes with the resignation; the other is a champion runner, he always catches him up.

I myself consider myself to be the most important figure in the world.
Idi Amin

In a few years people will be clinging to my coat tails to save the country.
Charles de Gaulle

It is, once again, as before, my duty to represent, to further – even, if the public safety should require it, to impose national interest on the nation ...
Charles de Gaulle

If we lose this war, I'll start another in my wife's name.
Moshe Dayan

Political power grows out of the barrel of a gun.
Mao Tse-Tung

He did not care in which direction the car was travelling, so long as he remained in the driving seat.
Lord Beaverbrook on Lloyd George

... he fancied he was walking on a red carpet that stretched into infinity.
Peggy Primrose, Horatio Bottomley's mistress

When I look back on all those worries I remember the story of an old man who said on his deathbed that he had had a lot of trouble in his life, most of which never happened.
Winston Churchill

Perhaps it is better to be irresponsible and right than responsible and wrong.
Winston Churchill

There are men who desire power simply for the sake of the happiness it will bring; these belong chiefly to political parties.
Nietzsche

The problem of power is ... how to get men of power to live *for* the public rather than *off* the public.
Robert F. Kennedy

Powerlessness frustrates; absolute powerlessness frustrates absolutely. Absolute frustration is a dangerous emotion to run a world with.
Russell Baker, The New York Times, 1969

Coining It

The lunatic fringe...
>*Theodore Roosevelt*, Autobiography

... government of the people, by the people, for the people...
>*Abraham Lincoln*, 19 November 1863

A week is a long time in politics...
>*Harold Wilson*, 1964

Indeed, let's be frank about it; some of our people have never had it so good...
>*Harold Macmillan*, 20 July 1957

... the little gnomes of Zürich.
>*Harold Wilson*, 12 November 1956

... the 'iron curtain'...
>*Viscountess Snowden*, 1920,
>later used by Goebbels and Churchill

'There is an iron curtain across Europe.'
>*St Vincent Troubridge*, Sunday Empire News,
>21 October 1945

We are all the President's men...
>*Henry Kissinger*

The iron maiden . . .
>> *Marjorie Proops*, Daily Mirror, 5 February 1975

. . . splendid isolation . . .
>> *Lord Goschen*, 26 February 1896

Speak for England.
>> *Leo Amery or Robert Boothby*

. . . the unpleasant and unacceptable face of capitalism.
>> *Edward Heath on Lonrho*, 20 May 1973

The only thing necessary for the triumph of evil is for good men to do nothing.
>> *Edmund Burke*

Like the Roman I seem to see 'the river Tiber foaming with much blood'.
>> *Enoch Powell*, Birmingham, 21 April 1968

Jaw-jaw is better than war-war.
>> *Harold Macmillan*, 30 January 1958

A spectre is haunting Europe – the spectre of Communism.
>> *The Communist Manifesto*, 1847

Better a three-day week than a no-day week.
>> *Edward Heath*, 28 July 1974

The business of America is business.
>> *Calvin Coolidge*

One man's wage increase is another man's price increase.
>> *Harold Wilson*, 11 January 1970

The world must be made safe for democracy.
>> *T. Woodrow Wilson*, 1917

Speak softly and carry a big stick...
Theodore Roosevelt, 1901

... the only thing we have to fear is fear itself.
Franklin Delano Roosevelt, 1933

You can fool all the people some of the time, but you cannot fool all the people all the time.
Abraham Lincoln, 1858

The lamps are going out all over Europe.
Viscount Grey of Falloden, 3 August 1914

His Majesty's Opposition...
John Cam Hobhouse, Baron Broughton

... a fit country for heroes to live in.
David Lloyd George

A Trap For Fools: Some Haunting Phrases

It does not mean, of course, that the pound here in Britain in your pocket... has been devalued.
> *Harold Wilson*, 20 November 1967

If you can bear to hear the truth you've spoken/ Twisted by knaves to make a trap for fools...
> *Harold Wilson quoting Kipling when asked by Edward Heath if he regretted the 'Pound in your Pocket' speech*

Taken to the streets, conflict is a destructive force; taken to the courts, conflict can be a creative force.
> *Richard M. Nixon*, 1971

There can be no whitewash in the White House.
> *Richard M. Nixon*, 30 April 1973

We need inequality in order to eliminate poverty.
> *Sir Keith Joseph*

The Conservatives do not believe it necessary and, even if it were, we should oppose it.
> *Lord Hailsham*

Let us begin by committing ourselves to the truth – to see it like it is...
> *Richard M. Nixon*, 1968

I don't give a shit what happens. I want you all to stonewall it. Let them plead the Fifth Amendment, cover up, or anything else if it'll save the plan.

Richard M. Nixon, on tape

The tragic lesson of guilty men walking free in this country has not been lost on the criminal community.

Richard M. Nixon

Nothing would please the Kremlin more than to have the people of this country choose a second-rate President.

Richard M. Nixon

The Language

In this despatch you have used every cliché known to the English language, except 'God is love' and 'Please adjust your dress before leaving'.
Winston Churchill admonishing the Foreign Office

... if thought corrupts language, language can also corrupt thought.
George Orwell, Politics and the English Language,
1946

This is an operative statement. The others are inoperative.
Richard Ziegler (Press Secretary to Richard M. Nixon, admitting that the White House had previously lied about its involvement in the Watergate break-in)

Political language – and with variations this is true of all political parties, from Conservatives to Anarchists – is designed to make lies sound truthful and murder respectable, and to give an appearance of solidity to pure wind.
George Orwell, Politics and the English Language,
1946

There are current plans for the use of American forces [in El Salvador] but the sterility of drawing lines around America's potential options constitutes the promulgation of roadways for those who are seeking to move against America's vital interests.

US State Department statement, New York Times, 8 February 1982

We are not at war with Egypt. We are in armed conflict.
Anthony Eden

Bonar Law: They tell me that we have to have what is called a slogan. What shall we have for this election?
Swinton: Well, I know what the country is feeling, they don't want to be buggered about.
Bonar Law: The sentiment is sound... let us call it 'Tranquillity'.

You can't find anything in a piss house now but political remarks.
Thwakhurst in Oliver St. John Gogarty's
As I Was Going Down Sackville Street

What we are trying to do is to go straight down the road in a four-dimensional situation.
Harold Wilson during Rhodesian negotiations

Few ideas are correct ones and what are correct no one can ascertain, but with words we govern men.
Disraeli, Contarini Fleming

You'll let a lot of wild horses out if you open this Pandora's box.

Ernest Bevin

Why can't you give me something more readable? It's so difficult to say.
Queen Elizabeth II, to her advisers on her speech for the opening of Parliament

To understand what ministers are sometimes saying you must buy a gobbledegook dictionary and add an arbitrary ten years to every promise they make.

Prince Philip

Man does not live by words alone, despite the fact that sometimes he has to eat them.

Adlai Stevenson

The most valuable of all talents is that of never using two words when one will do.

Thomas Jefferson

A candidate for office can have no greater advantage than muddled syntax; no greater liability than a command of the language.

Marya Manners, More in Anger, 1958

In modern life nothing produces such an effect as a good platitude. It makes the whole world kin.

Oscar Wilde, An Ideal Husband

House Work

The British, being brought up on team games, enter their House of Commons in the spirit of those who would rather be doing something else.

C. Northcote Parkinson

To Westminster Hall, where the Hall full of people to see the issues of the day, the King being to come to speak to the House today. One extraordinary thing was this day, a man, a Quaker, came naked through the Hall, only very civilly tied about the privities to avoid scandal, and with a chafing dish of fire and brimstone burning upon his head did pass through the Hall crying 'Repent! Repent!'

Samuel Pepys, Diary, 29 July 1667

I had better recall, before someone else does, that I said on one occasion that all was fair in love, war and parliamentary procedure.

Michael Foot

The human brain starts working the moment you are born and never stops until you stand up to speak in public.

Sir George Jessel

The Commons listens with great humility to humbugs and compliments them on their sincerity. It hates to hear awkward truths and abuses those who tell them. It suffers fools, particularly the sentimental, gladly.

Woodrow Wyatt

This place is the longest running farce in the West End.
Cyril Smith

... we were in hopes to have had a vote this day in our favour, and so the generality of the House was; but my speech being so long, many had gone out to dinner and come in again half drunk...
Samuel Pepys, Diary, 5 March 1668

More and more debate, where it is not actually curtailed, is becoming a ritual dance, interspersed with cat-calls.
Lord Hailsham

A speech is like a love affair. Any fool can start it, but to end it requires considerable skill.
Lord Mancroft

I have hardly ever had to make an important speech without feeling violently sick most of the day before...
Harold Macmillan

I stand up when he nudges me. I sits down when they pull my coat.
Ernest Bevin

If you like life and the human circus it is hard not to like the House of Commons.
Woodrow Wyatt

I was sent to this place to vote with my head, not with my feet.
Winston Churchill, replying to an accusation that he had gone to the 'wrong' lobby and voted against his party

Let thy speech be short, comprehending much in a few words.
Ecclesiasticus 32:8

Party Time

I often think it's comical
How nature always does contrive
That every boy and every gal
That's born into the world alive
Is either a little Liberal
Or else a little Conservative.

W. S. Gilbert, Iolanthe, 1882

Where there are political parties each party finds the source of such evils in the fact that the opposing party, instead of itself, is at the helm of State.

Karl Marx

Liberalism is trust of the people tempered by prudence; Conservatism is distrust of the people tempered by fear.

W. E. Gladstone

A man who is not a Liberal at sixteen has no heart; a man who is not a Conservative at sixty has no head.

Benjamin Disraeli

Of the hundreds of resolutions I have seen passed by Labour conferences outlining a drastic programme of reform I can hardly call one to mind which has had any political effect. Conferences will talk, let them talk.

Philip Snowden, Labour minister

You Liberals think that goats are just sheep from broken homes.

> *Malcolm Bradbury and Christopher Bigsby,*
> After Dinner Game

A Conservative government is an organized hypocrisy.

> *Benjamin Disraeli*

Liberal – a power worshipper without power.

> *George Orwell*

Conservative, n. a statesman who is enamoured of existing evils, as distinguished from a Liberal, who wishes to replace them with others.

> *Ambrose Bierce*

They are mostly men of laborious habits, teetotallers, of intellectual interests, with a belief in the reasonableness of mankind. The English working man is not a teetotaller, has little respect for intellectual interests and does not in the least degree trouble himself about the reasonableness of mankind.

> *C. F. G. Masterman, on the Parliamentary*
> *Labour Party of 1909*

A party dominated by second-class brewers and company promotors – a Casino capitalism – is not likely to represent anybody but itself.

> *Harold Macmillan on the Tory party of the*
> *Baldwin era*

It is a bizarre biological fact that the Conservative Party can be directed along a sensible left-wing path only by a leader with impeccable aristocratic connections.

> *Humphrey Berkeley*

I am neither Whig nor Tory. My politics are described in one word, and that word is England.

> *Benjamin Disraeli*

The party is a moral crusade . . .

Harold Wilson

If God had been a Liberal there wouldn't have been ten commandments, there would have been ten suggestions.

Malcolm Bradbury and Christopher Bigsby,
After Dinner Game

If I had founded the Party, I should not have put out any programme at all.

Joseph Goebbels

All political parties die at last of swallowing their own lies.

John Arbuthnot, 1667–1735

Even more important than winning an election is governing the nation. That is the test of a political party – the acid, final test.

Adlai Stevenson

Left Hooks

Political toleration is a by-product of the complacency of the ruling class. When that complacency is disturbed there never was a more bloody-minded set of thugs than the British ruling class.

Michael Foot

They are nothing else but a load of kippers, two-faced with no guts.

Eric Heffer on the Tories

Conservatives are not necessarily stupid, but most stupid people are conservatives.

John Stuart Mill

Every time Mr Macmillan comes back from abroad Mr Butler goes to the airport and grips him warmly by the throat.

Harold Wilson

A conservative is a man who sits and thinks, mostly sits.

Woodrow Wilson

No attempt at ethical or social seduction can eradicate from my heart a deep burning hatred for the Tory Party ... So far as I am concerned they are lower than vermin.

Aneurin Bevan

... we are arguing about the future; they seek only to consolidate the past.

Harold Wilson on Harold Macmillan's Government

Tories are not always wrong, but they are always wrong at the right moment.

Lady Violet Bonham-Carter

I am sure Mr Heath thinks he is honest. But I wish he didn't have to have his friends say it so often.

Roy Jenkins

Their Europeanism is nothing but imperialism with an inferiority complex.

Denis Healey on the Conservative Party

A conservative is a man with two perfectly good legs who, however, has never learned how to walk forward.

Franklin Delano Roosevelt

The modern conservative is engaged in one of man's oldest exercises in moral philosophy, that is the search for superior moral justification for selfishness ... The conspicuously wealthy turn up urging the character-building value of privation for the poor.

J. K. Galbraith

For the first time for a long time we have a government, many of whose members regard the Queen as a social inferior.

Simon Hoggart on Margaret Thatcher's Government

Right Crosses

Though I never shout at Labour members or insult them, I can never understand the psychology of some of our men who . . . endeavoured to reason with them.

Neville Chamberlain

I do not often attack the Labour Party. They do it so well themselves.

Edward Heath

In close-up the British revolutionary Left seethes with such repulsive, self-righteous dogmatists that it practically drives one to enlist as a deck hand on 'Morning Cloud'.

Richard Neville

They are going about the country stirring up complacency.

William Whitelaw on Labour ministers during the October 1974 General Election

What a genius the Labour Party has for cutting itself in half and letting the two parts writhe in public.

'Cassandra' (Sir William Connor)

As with the Christian religion, the worst advertisement for Socialism is its adherents.

George Orwell, The Road to Wigan Pier

The Middle Ground

We know what happens to people who stay in the middle of the road. They get run over.

Aneurin Bevan

If the fence is strong enough I'll sit on it.

Cyril Smith

The Right Honourable Gentleman has sat so long on the fence that the iron has entered his soul.

Lloyd George to Sir John Simon

The middle of the road is all of the usable surface. The extremes, right and left, are in the gutters.

Dwight D. Eisenhower

I am on the right wing of the middle of the road with a strong radical bias.

Tony Benn

England does not love coalitions.

Benjamin Disraeli

All government... is founded on compromise and barter.

Edmund Burke

The inherent vice of capitalism is the unequal sharing of blessings; the inherent virtue of socialism is the equal sharing of miseries.

Winston Churchill

An independent is the guy who wants to take the politics out of politics.

Adlai Stevenson

Cruel Cuts & Cold Steel

The blows of a whip raise a welt, but a blow of the tongue crushes bones.

Ecclesiasticus 28:17

Like a cushion he always bore the impress of the last man who sat on him.

Lloyd George on Lord Derby

If a traveller were informed that such a man was Leader of the House of Commons he may well begin to comprehend how the Egyptians worshipped an insect.

Benjamin Disraeli on Lord John Russell

When they circumcised Herbert Samuel they threw away the wrong bit.

Lloyd George

Reminds me of nothing so much as a dead fish before it has time to stiffen.

George Orwell on Clement Attlee

The trouble with Senator Long is that he is suffering from halitosis of the intellect. That's assuming Emperor Long has an intellect.

Harold L. Ickes

Q: How can you tell when he's lying?
A: When his lips are moving.
> BBC TV's That Was The Week That Was
> on Harold Wilson

It was announced that the touble was not malignant . . .
I remarked that it was a typical triumph of modern
science to find the only part of Randolph that was not
malignant and remove it.
> Evelyn Waugh on Randolph Churchill's lung
> operation

Like being savaged by a dead sheep.
> Denis Healey on criticism from Geoffrey Howe

He always played the game and always lost it.
> said of Sir Austen Chamberlain

A desiccated calculating machine.
> Aneurin Bevan on Hugh Gaitskill

A sophistical rhetorician inebriated with the exuber-
ance of his own verbosity.
> Disraeli on Gladstone

Rather than go through with that again . . . I would
prefer to have three or four of my teeth out.
> Adolf Hitler to Mussolini about a meeting with Franco

He saw foreign policy through the wrong end of a
municipal drainpipe.
> Lloyd George on Neville Chamberlain

He is not only a bore but he bores for England.
> Malcolm Muggeridge on Sir Anthony Eden

. . . the most extraordinary objet d'art our society has
ever produced.
> J. M. Keynes on Arthur Balfour

Lord Birkenhead is very clever, but sometimes his brains go to his head.

Margot Asquith

He can compress the most words into the smallest idea of any man I ever met.
Abraham Lincoln on one of his political enemies

He could not see a belt without hitting below it.
Margot Asquith on Lloyd George

Dr Rhodes Boyson might also clamber back into his Cruikshank engraving and return to whichever unpublished Dickens novel he appears in.
Simon Hoggart

He was brilliant to the top of his army boots.
Lloyd George on Field Marshal Haig

Like Odysseus he looked wiser when seated.
J. M. Keynes on Woodrow Wilson

He would sooner keep hot coals in his mouth than a witticism.
Bonar Law on F. E. Smith, Earl of Birkenhead

A man . . . of the utmost insignificance.
Curzon on Stanley Baldwin

I met Curzon in Downing Street from whom I got the sort of greeting a corpse would give to an undertaker.
Stanley Baldwin

They asked for a leader and were given a public relations officer.
Malcolm Muggeridge on Sir Anthony Eden

It is fitting that we should have buried the Unknown

Prime Minister by the side of the Unknown Soldier.
Earl Asquith on Bonar Law

Alexander Haig: a banality wrapped in a platitude inside a tautology.

Anon

Disraeli did have a vision... an unimaginative approach can grip people.
Edward Heath to his biographer, Margaret Laing

One morning they opened their papers and read that Lloyd George had said of Bonar Law that he was 'honest to the point of simplicity'. And they said 'By God, that is what we have been looking for.'
Stanley Baldwin

Benn flung himself into the Sixties technology with the enthusiasm (not to say language) of a newly enrolled Boy Scout demonstrating knot-tying to his indulgent parents.

Bernard Levin

There is no reason to attack the monkey when the organ-grinder is present.
Aneurin Bevan referring to Selwyn Lloyd and Harold Macmillan

The Noel Coward of international politics.
Charles Graves on Anthony Eden

They elevated inactivity into a principle and feebleness into a virtue.
Harold Macmillan on Stanley Baldwin and Ramsay MacDonald

Margaret Thatcher ... has one great advantage – she is a daughter of the people and looks trim, as the daughters of the people desire to be. Shirley Williams has such an advantage over her because she's a member of the upper-middle class and can achieve the kitchen-sink-revolutionary look that one cannot get unless one has been to a really good school.

Dame Rebecca West to Jilly Cooper

His rather odd accent... a mixture of rural Kent and Wodehousean Oxford.

Edward Heath described by his ex-sister-in-law

... he appeared honourably ineligible for the struggle of life.

Cyril Connolly on Alec Douglas-Home in
Enemies of Promise

If he ever went to school without any boots it was because he was too big for them.

Ivor Bulmer-Thomas on Harold Wilson

Churchill: Swapping Punches

There but for the grace of God, goes God.
on Sir Stafford Cripps

So they told me how Mr Gladstone read Homer for fun,
which I thought served him right.
My Early Life

Mr Attlee combines a limited outlook with strong
qualities of resistance.

In defeat unbeatable; in victory unbearable.
on Field Marshal Montgomery

The difference between him and Arthur is that Arthur is
wicked and moral, Asquith is good and immoral.
on Asquith and Arthur Balfour

He is a sheep in wolf's clothing.
on Clement Attlee

He is a modest little man with much to be modest about.
on Clement Attlee

It is a fine thing to be honest but it is also important to
be right.

on Stanley Baldwin

Buller was a characteristic British personality. He looked stolid. He said little, and what he said was obscure.

on Sir Redvers Buller in My early Life

Winston has devoted the best years of his life to preparing his impromptu speeches.

F. E. Smith

Simply a radio personality who outlived his prime.
Evelyn Waugh

He is a man suffering from petrified adolescence.
Aneurin Bevan

Demolitions

I have waited fifty years to see the Boneless Wonder sitting on the Treasury Bench.

Winston Churchill on Ramsay MacDonald

He had sufficient conscience to bother him, but not sufficient to keep him straight.

Lloyd George on Ramsay MacDonald

Sit down man. You're a bloody tragedy.

James Maxton to Ramsay MacDonald in the House of Commons

Nixon is a purposeless man, but I have great faith in his cowardice.

Jimmy Breslin

Richard Nixon is a no-good lying bastard. He can lie out of both sides of his mouth at the same time, and even if he caught himself telling the truth, he'd lie just to keep his hand in.

President Harry Truman

You don't set a fox to watch the chickens just because he has a lot of experience in the hen house.

President Harry Truman on Richard M. Nixon

Coolidge is a better example of evolution than either Bryan or Darrow, for he knows when not to talk, which is the biggest asset the monkey possesses over the human.

Will Rogers

How can they tell?
Dorothy Parker, when told that President Coolidge was dead

Jerry Ford is a nice guy, but he played too much football with his helmet off.

Lyndon Johnson

Jerry Ford is so dumb that he can't fart and chew gum at the same time.

Lyndon Johnson

A year ago Gerald Ford was unknown throughout America, now he is unknown throughout the world.
The Guardian, August 1974

Sword-Play

If it's a boy I'll call him John. If it's a girl I'll call her
Mary. But if, as I suspect, it's only wind, I'll call it F. E.
Smith.

> *Lord Chief Justice Hewart's riposte to F. E. Smith*
> *who had commented on the impressive size of the*
> *judge's stomach by asking,*
> *'What's it to be – a boy or a girl?'*

Winston Churchill: There are two things I revere above
all: God and the House of Commons.
Sir Stafford Cripps: I hope you treat God better than
you do the House of Commons.

Labour MP (of Herbert Morrison): Of course, the
trouble with Herbie is, he's his own worst enemy.
Ernest Bevin: Not while I'm alive he ain't.

Bessie Braddock MP: You're drunk!
Churchill: And you, madam, are ugly. But I shall be
sober in the morning.

In the course of his speech he uses the phrase, *primus
inter pares*. The Labour people cry out 'Translate!'
Winston without a moment's hesitation goes on,
'Certainly I shall translate' – then he pauses and turns to
the right – 'for the benefit of any old Etonians who may
be present.'

> *Harold Nicolson*, Diary, 22 January 1941

Harold Wilson: After half a century of democratic advance the whole process has ground to a halt with a 14th Earl.

Sir Alec Douglas-Home: I suppose Mr Wilson, when you come to think of it, is the 14th Mr Wilson.

Winston, if I were married to you, I'd put poison in your coffee.

Nancy, if you were my wife I'd drink it.

Nancy, Viscountess Astor to Winston Churchill

I think that the issues we are trying to debate are a little beyond the comprehension of the pedantic grammarian. We are all extremely fond of the hon. Gentleman, and enjoy his interruptions, but I sometimes think that if the world were ever practically destroyed by a nuclear explosion, the hon. Gentleman would creep out of his shell next morning, if, happily, he were preserved, and complain that somebody had split an infinitive.

Harold Wilson to Sir Kenneth Pickthorne during a debate on nuclear arms for Germany, 3 July 1963

Yes, Margaret, but it takes me much longer to change than it does you.

Norman St John Stevas when asked by the Prime Minister, Margaret Thatcher, why he was leaving early from a Cabinet meeting in order to attend a function which she too was to attend

Echoes

Lord Salisbury and myself have brought you peace –
but a peace I hope with honour.
Benjamin Disraeli, July 1878

I believe it is peace in our time... peace with honour.
Neville Chamberlain, October 1938

It is not fit that you should sit here any longer... you
shall now give your place to better men.
Oliver Cromwell to the 'Rump Parliament',
22 January 1654

You have sat too long here for any good you have been
doing. Depart I say and let us have done with you. In the
name of God go!
Leo Amery to Neville Chamberlain, May 1940

This country will not be a good place for any of us to
live in unless we make it a good place for all of us to live
in.

Theodore Roosevelt

This land of ours cannot be a good place for any of us to
live in unless it is a good place for all of us to live in.
Richard M. Nixon

Getting It Wrong

When the President does it, that means it's not illegal.
Richard M. Nixon

The cumulative effects of the economic and financial sanctions might well bring the rebellion to an end within a matter of weeks rather than months.
Harold Wilson, January 1966, *on Rhodesia*

I don't believe in black majority rule ever in Rhodesia...
not in a thousand years.
Ian Smith, March 1976

In all the years of public life I have never obstructed justice... your President is no crook!
Richard M. Nixon

I have often been accused of putting my foot in my mouth, but I have never put my hand in your pocket.
Spiro T. Agnew

After all, they are only going into their own back garden.
Lord Lothian on Hitler's reoccupation of the Rhineland

I often think how much easier the world would have been to manage if Herr Hitler and Signor Mussolini had been at Oxford.

Lord Halifax, November 1937

He may be a blackguard, but not a dirty blackguard.

Sir Neville Henderson on Goering

I'm forty-three years old, and I'm the healthiest candidate for the president in the United States. You've travelled with me enough to know that I'm not going to die in office.

John F. Kennedy

We cannot change our policies now. After all we are not political whores.

Mussolini

Hitler has missed the bus.

Neville Chamberlain during the Phoney War

Guy Burgess comes to see me, and I tell him there is no chance now of his being sent to Moscow.

Harold Nicolson, Diary, 29 July 1940

I believe that men are beginning to see, not perhaps the golden age, but an age which at any rate is brightening from decade to decade, and will lead us some time to an elevation from which we can see the things for which the heart of mankind is longing.

President Woodrow Wilson, 1918

Hitting the Nail

Macmillan: Well, of course, you can have a war and then what will happen? You will be killed, I shall be killed, my country will be wiped out, most of your country will be wiped out and what will be left?
Khrushchev: I'll tell you what will be left, a number of Africans and a lot of Chinese.

I owe nothing to Women's Lib.

Margaret Thatcher

I hear that whenever anyone in the White House tells a lie Nixon gets a royalty.

Richard M. Nixon

According to the English there are two countries in the world today which are led by adventurers: Germany and Italy ... Today she is ruled merely by incompetents.

Hitler to Ciano

If anyone is crazy enough to want to kill the president of the United States, he can do it. All he must be prepared to do is give his life for the president's.

John F. Kennedy

There are few virtues which the Poles do not possess and there are few errors they have avoided.

Winston Churchill, 1945

Either back us or sack us.

*James Callaghan to the electorate before the
1977 General Election*

That is not executive privilege. It is executive
poppycock.
Senator Sam Ervin during the Watergate hearings, 1973

Is the ownership of the world to be stereotyped by
perpetual tenure in the hands of those who possess the
different territories today?... The world continues to
offer glittering prizes to those who have stout arms and
sharp swords, and it is therefore extremely improbable
that the experience of future nations will differ in any
material respect from that which has happened since
the twilight of the human race.

Lord Birkenhead (F. E. Smith), 1923

Achieving

Nothing matters very much, and very few things matter at all.

Arthur Balfour

The true men of action in our time, those who transform the world, are not the politicians and statesmen, but the scientists.

W. H. Auden, The Dyer's Hand

He spent his declining years trying to guess the answer to the Irish question. Unfortunately whenever he was getting warm, the Irish secretly changed the question.

Sellar & Yeatman, on Gladstone in 1066 and All That

There used to be a limitation on the number of false teeth a recruit could have. I have removed that limitation.

Leslie Hore-Belisha, November 1937

Many of our troubles are due to the fact that our people turn to politicians for everything.

Margaret Thatcher

We are not in politics to ignore people's worries; we are in politics to deal with them.

Margaret Thatcher

How can anyone govern a nation that has two hundred and forty-six different kinds of cheese?

Charles de Gaulle

I ask you to judge me by the enemies I have made.

Franklin Delano Roosevelt

I believe we would turn out much better work in the

House of Commons if we did two hours' digging every day.

Lloyd George

If half the people who make speeches would make concrete floors they would be doing more good.

Lord Darling

No more distressing moment can ever face a British government than that which requires it to come to a hard and fast and specific decision.

Barbara Tuchman, The Guns of August

There are two problems in my life. The political ones are insoluble and the economic ones are incomprehensible.

Sir Alec Douglas-Home

I have no doubt we will get out of the recession some time. When we do, no doubt the Prime Minister and others will tell us it is the greatest miracle since the loaves and fishes.

Michael Foot

In this world nothing can be said to be certain, except death and taxes.

Benjamin Franklin

In the long run we are all dead.

J. M. Keynes

In the end it may well be that Britain will be honoured by the historians more for the way she disposed of an empire than for the way in which she acquired it.

David Ormsby Gore, British Ambassador to the USA,
1962

How small, of all the ills that men endure,
The part which Kings or States can cure.

Samuel Johnson

True Confessions

I'm a Ford, not a Lincoln.

Gerald Ford

I'm not a lovable man.

Richard M. Nixon

Keith and I have no toes.
Margaret Thatcher referring to Sir Keith Joseph

I don't give a damn about protocol. I'm a swinger.
Bring out the beautiful spies.

Henry Kissinger

I can't take dictation. I can't type. I can't even answer
the phone.
*Elizabeth Ray, Washington secretary to
Congressman Wayne Hays*

I love idleness so much and so dearly, that I have hardly
the heart to say a word against it...

Charles James Fox

Don't underestimate the ability of party politicians to
find alibis.

Michael Heseltine

I didn't ought never to have done it.
Ernest Bevin who, as Foreign Secretary, gave
official recognition to Communist China

If I am a great man, then a good many of the great men in history are frauds.
Andrew Bonar Law

My only great qualification for being put in charge of the Navy is that I am very much at sea.
Sir Edward Carson on being made responsible for
naval affairs in the Coalition Government of 1916

Dontopedology

Oh no thank you, I only smoke on special occasions.
> *Labour minister when offered a cigar by*
> *King George VI*

Shot any dogs lately?
> *Cyril Smith to Jeremy Thorpe, 1976*

He is used to dealing with estate workers. I cannot see
how anyone can say he is out of touch.
> *Lady Caroline Douglas-Home,*
> *Sir Alec Douglas-Home's daughter*

The President of Israel.
> *Gerald Ford proposing a toast to Anwar Sadat*

To some extent, if you've seen one city slum you've seen
them all.
> *Spiro T. Agnew*

When Britain is about to enter the EEC it is somewhat
tactless to print on the back of the £5 note a picture of
British gunners blowing the French army to blazes and
accompanying it with a large portrait of the Duke of
Wellington.
> *Lord Leatherhead, 1972*

In Victory

What a day! Two salmon this morning and the offer of
the Exchequer this afternoon.

Neville Chamberlain

Indeed you won the election, but I won the count.

Anastasio Somoza, dictator of Nicaragua

However tired people may be of me, I think that most
people in the country will regard me as the lesser of two
evils. I always put these things in a modest way.

Harold Wilson, 26 April 1970

Tomorrow every Duchess in London will be wanting to
kiss me!

*Ramsay MacDonald, on forming the National
Government*

In Defeat

A funny thing happened to me on the way to the White House.
Adlai Stevenson, defeated in the presidential election
1966

A wretched, disheartening result. And a little mouse shall lead them.
Hugh Dalton, on Attlee's winning the leadership
of the Labour party, 1935

... the man who is running the Government one day was sped on his way the next, with just about as much ceremony as a shop assistant found with his hand in the till.
Marcia Williams, on Harold Wilson's defeat, 1970

It gives to the workings of democracy the dramatic immediacy of a *coup d'état*, with removal vans in place of machine guns.
Anthony Sampson, The New Anatomy of Britain,
on the evacuation of Number 10 by a defeated
prime minister

Well, Al, there goes the presidency!
Richard M. Nixon to Alexander Haig during
Watergate, July 1974

I brought myself down. I gave them a sword. And they stuck it in. And they twisted it with relish. And, I guess, if I'd been in their position, I'd have done the same thing!

Richard M. Nixon

You won't have Nixon to kick around any more, gentlemen. This is my last press conference.
Richard M. Nixon, 2 November 1962

I am convinced that we have a degree of delight, and that no small one, in the real misfortunes and pains of others.

Edmund Burke

The opportunity to sleep nine hours a night and really relax has been extremely good for me. I ask you to disabuse yourself of any idea that prison is harmful.
John Stonehouse

I let down my friends, I let down my country. I let down our system of government.
Richard M. Nixon, 1977

There comes a time in every man's life when he must make way for an older man.
*Reginald Maudling,
on being dropped from the Shadow Cabinet*

Horatio Bottomley, in prison, sewing mail bags:
   Visitor: 'Ah, Bottomley, sewing?'
   Bottomley: 'No, reaping.'

Magnanimity

... and then he took off his glasses and grinned round at
the Conservative benches. 'We are a decent lot,' he said,
beaming upon them. Then he swung round and leant
forward over the box right into the faces of the Labour
people: 'All of us, the whole nation.'
>   *Harold Nicolson describing Winston Churchill,*
>   November 1944

He [Chamberlain] ends with a fierce denunciation of
the Germans for invading Holland and Belgium. It is a
magnificent statement, and all the hatred that I have felt
for Chamberlain subsides as if a piece of bread were
dropped into a glass of champagne.
>   *Harold Nicolson,* Diary, 10 May 1940

Magnanimity in politics is not seldom the truest
wisdom; and a great empire and little minds go ill
together.

>   *Edmund Burke*

Say That Again

Personnel selection is decisive. People are our most valuable capital.

Josef Stalin

I have never delivered a firebrand speech.

Adolf Hitler, 1933

I am not nor ever have been, a man of the right. My position was on the left and is now in the centre of politics.

Sir Oswald Mosley, 26 April 1968

I never knew the lower classes had such white skins.

Lord Curzon (attrib.)

My entry into the spring industry was not accompanied by any fanfares.

Cyril Smith, Big Cyril

Actually I vote Labour, but my butler's a Tory.

Lord Mountbatten to a Tory canvasser, 1945

... to evolve policies from ideas, to organize mass movements, to campaign for these policies, to convince the people to accept them, to carry through the programme by consent, lubricating the process with wise compromises without losing sight of the objective as he goes along – these are the tasks of the politician.

Tony Benn, 20 March 1964

All the world over, I will back the masses against the classes.

William Gladstone, 28 June 1886

Corruption at home, aggression abroad, sentiment by the bucketful, patriotism by the Imperial pint, the open hand at the public Exchequer and the open door at the public house, dear food for the million, cheap labour for the millionaire.

Winston Churchill on the Edwardian Tory party

We Germans, who are the only people in the world who have a decent attitude towards animals, will also assume a decent attitude towards these human animals.

Heinrich Himmler, 4 October 1943

Getting Heavy

I never give them hell. I just tell the truth and they think it's hell.

Harry S. Truman

First, ah'm gonna give you a two-minute lecture on integrity, and then ah'm gonna ruin you.

Lyndon Johnson, to a transgressing politician

Si vous m'opposerez, je vous liquiderai.
Churchill to de Gaulle, from Harold Nicolson's Diary,
5 July 1943

Loyal and Loving Friends

In politics . . . shared hatreds are almost always the basis
of friendships.

Alexis de Tocqueville

A friend in need is a friend to be avoided.

Lord Samuel

Greater love hath no man than this, that he lay down
his friends for his life.

Jeremy Thorpe

. . . in dismissing Mr Powell, Mr Heath takes the known
risk of having Mr Powell as an enemy; that fortunately
is less grave than the risk of having Mr Powell as a
colleague.

Times *leader*, 9 February 1968

When it comes to the dirty work, they are pure Chicago.
Walter Terry, the Sun, 11 May 1976,
on Liberal MPs' attitudes during the Thorpe affair

I feel as loyal today to the President I served as I ever
have . . .
    I've no reason to defend Nixon on drinking, but I
must speak the truth, and that truth is: in all my years
with him as candidate or as President, I never saw him
intoxicated. The problem was he didn't *need* to drink to
excess to start losing his faculties and appear foolish.
H. R. Haldeman, The Ends of Power

She looks like an angel cake, but God help Heath.
>*Jean Rook on Margaret Thatcher before she was*
>*elected leader of the Conservative Party*

I wouldn't say she was open-minded on the Middle East so much as empty headed. For instance, she probably thinks that Sinai is the plural of sinuses.
>*Jonathan Aitken MP on Margaret Thatcher*

I would walk over my grandmother if necessary to get Nixon re-elected.
>*Charles Colson, Special Counsel to the President*

This fellow Deane is a conceited fellow and one that means the King a great deal of service; but however, I learn much of him and he is, I perceive, of great use to the King in his place, and so I shall give him all the encouragement I can.
>*Samuel Pepys*, Diary, 6 June 1963

I'd much rather have the fellow inside my tent pissing out, than outside my tent pissing in.
>*Lyndon Johnson explaining why he kept*
>*J. Edgar Hoover on at the FBI*

Bugger the Prime Minister's luggage.
>*Bill Houseden, Harold Wilson's chauffeur, reluctant*
>*to climb aboard HMS* Fearless *from a small launch*
>*in high seas with Wilson's boxes and baggage*

Anyone who extends him the right hand of fellowship is in danger of losing a couple of fingers.
>*Alva Johnson on Mayor La Guardia of New York*

I never trust a man unless I've got his pecker in my pocket.
>*Lyndon Johnson*

My Hero

I think it's the most extraordinary collection of talent... that has ever been gathered together at the White House – with the possible exception of when Thomas Jefferson dined alone.
John F. Kennedy at a dinner for Nobel Prize Winners,
29 April 1962

The first time you meet Winston you see all his faults and the rest of your life you spend in discovering his virtues.
Lady Lytton on Winston Churchill

In Franklin Roosevelt there died the greatest American friend we have ever known and the greatest champion of freedom who has ever brought help and comfort from the New World to the Old.
Winston Churchill

The last time I was in this hall was when my late beloved boss, Frank Knox, the Secretary of the Navy, spoke here, and it was a better speech he gave than the one I'll be giving tonight. I know. I wrote them both.
Adlai Stevenson

He would cry over the death of a swan or a cat. For human life he had little regard, least of all for his own.
Lord Boothby on Winston Churchill

War was his element and Power his objective.
> *Lord Boothby on Winston Churchill*

To have been alive with him was to have dined at the table of history.
> *'Cassandra' (Sir William Conner) on Churchill*

Then comes Winston with his hundred-horse-power mind and what can I do?
> *Stanley Baldwin*

Then Lloyd George gets up and makes a moving speech telling Winston how fond he is of him. Winston cries slightly and mops his eyes.
> *Harold Nicolson*, Diary, 13 May 1940

Top Dogs

In America any boy may become President and I suppose that is just one of the risks he runs.
Adlai Stevenson

A good character is not merely unnecessary for becoming Prime Minister. It may be positively harmful to its owner.
Woodrow Wyatt, Turn Again, Westminster

There are three classes which need sanctuary more than others – birds, wild flowers and Prime Ministers.
Stanley Baldwin

When I was a boy I was told that anybody could become President; I'm beginning to believe it.
Clarence Darrow

It wasn't an election. It was an assumption.
Norman St John Stevas on Margaret Thatcher's election as Conservative Party Leader

The first essential for a Prime Minister is to be a good butcher.
William Gladstone

If you are as happy, my dear sir, on entering this house

as I am in leaving it and returning home, you are the happiest man in the country.

James Buchanan to his successor, Abraham Lincoln

I don't know anything about being President. I just found out today how to be vice-president.

Alexander Throttlebottom

Lord Rosebery... by marrying a Rothschild, being Prime Minister and winning the Derby demonstrated that it was possible to improve one's financial status and run the Empire without neglecting the study of form.

Claud Cockburn, A Good Time Had

I had rather be right than be President.

Henry Clay

Scrubbing floors and emptying bedpans has as much dignity as the Presidency.

Richard M. Nixon

I don't know. It would depend to some extent on the woman, wouldn't it? What I do know is that a man who got married in order to be a better Prime Minister wouldn't be either a good Prime Minister or a good husband.

Edward Heath to Margaret Laing, when asked if he would be a better Prime Minister if married

There is something utterly nauseating about a system of society which pays a harlot 25 times as much as it pays its Prime Minister...

Harold Wilson, 1963

I believe the greatest asset a head of state can have is the ability to get a good night's sleep.

Harold Wilson

It was a supreme expression of the mediocrity of the apparatus that Stalin himself rose to his position.

Trotsky, My Life

... the atmosphere inside usually is reminiscent of a cloister. There is a feeling that you have been cut off from the outside world. No. 10 is more of a monastery than a power house.

Marcia Williams, Inside No. 10

When we were at Downing Street their favourite dish seemed to be stew. We knew this because one could smell the stew over a large part of the building. Before we went to No. 10 people often used to refer to the sweet smell of success. I never realized that the predominant smell of political success would turn out to be the messengers' stew.

Marcia Williams, Inside No. 10,
on the messengers' practice of cooking their own meals

Questioner: Mr Butler, would you say that this is the best Prime Minister we have?
R. A. B. Butler: Yes.

Butler on Macmillan's premiership

The Fourth Estate

... in the Reporters' Gallery yonder, there sat a Fourth Estate, more important far than they all.

Thomas Carlyle

Have you heard? The Prime Minister [Lloyd George] has resigned and Northcliffe has sent for the King.

popular joke, 1919

The Government has been faced with an orchestrated campaign of pressures by the newspapers. They even had the gargantuan intellect of Bernard Levin squeaking away in the undergrowth like a demented vole.

Dennis Healey, 13 June 1976

By office boys for office boys.

Lord Salisbury on the Daily Mail

An editor is one who separates the wheat from the chaff and prints the chaff.

Adlai Stevenson

Do you agree, Mr President, to Watergate becoming... the fourth show?

David Frost, while planning the Frost-Nixon interviews, to Richard Nixon

What the proprietorship of these papers is aiming at is power, and power without responsibility – the prerogative of the harlot throughout history.

Stanley Baldwin on Lords Beaverbrook and Rothermere (Duke of Devonshire: 'Good God, that's done it. He's lost us the tarts' vote.')

If I rescued a child from drowning, the Press would no doubt headline the story 'Benn grabs child'.

Tony Benn, 2 March 1975

I don't make jokes – I just watch the government and report the facts.

Will Rogers

The Civil Service

A difficulty for every solution.
Lord Samuel (attrib.) on the Civil Service

You can cut any public expenditure except the Civil
Service; those lads spent a hundred years learning to
look after themselves.
Sir Richard Marsh, 1976

We to a committee of the Council to discourse
concerning pressing of men; but Lord how they meet;
never sit down – one comes, now another goes, then
comes another – one complaining that nothing is done,
another swearing that he hath been there these two
hours and nobody came. At last it came to this: my Lord
Annesly, says he, 'I think we must be forced to get the
King to come to every committee, for I do not see that we
do anything, at any time but when he is here.'
Samuel Pepys, Diary, 27 February 1665

Members rise from CMG (known sometimes in
Whitehall as 'Call me God') to KCMG ('Kindly call me
God') to ... the GCMG ('God calls me God').
Anthony Sampson, The Anatomy of Britain

Up and to my office, where busy all the morning.
Particularly, setting my people to work in transcribing

pieces of letters public and private, which I do collect against a black day, to defend the office with and myself.
Samuel Pepys, Diary, 17 June 1667

With Sir J. Mennes to Whitehall, where met by W. Batten and Lord Brounker, to attend the King and Duke of York at the cabinet; but nobody had determined what to speak of, but only in general to ask for money.
Samuel Pepys, Diary, 7 October 1666

The Civil Service is a self-perpetuating oligarchy, and what better system is there?
Lord Armstrong, head of the Civil Service, 1977

There is only one man who has ever made the Treasury do what it didn't want to do. That was Lloyd George. There will never be another.
P. J. Grigg, as told to Lord Boothby

A situation in a public office is secure, but laborious and mechanical, and without the two great springs of life, Hope and Fear.
William Hazlitt

The State, in choosing men to serve it takes no notice of their opinions. If they be willing faithfully to serve it, that satisfies.
Oliver Cromwell

The Lords

When I want a peerage, I shall buy one like an honest man.

Lord Northcliffe (attrib.)

Think of it, a second chamber selected by the whips – a seraglio of eunuchs!

Michael Foot, 1969

I went to the Lords because I had nowhere else to go.

Lord Shinwell, 1977

We are nothing much to look at and most of us are not very young any more. We are not very exciting to listen to and many of us are not great orators, but we do have dignity.

Lord Denham, 1975

I wonder what you thought of the Honours List. I have never ceased to congratulate myself that I did not figure among that rabble.

Neville Chamberlain, 1918

Every man has a House of Lords in his own head. Fears, prejudices, misconceptions – those are the peers...

Lloyd George, 1927

For the first time I was aware of that layer of blubber which encases an English peer, the sediment of permanent adulation.

Cyril Connolly, Enemies of Promise

I accepted a peerage through a combination of the coincidence of circumstances leading to an aberration.

Lord Briginshaw, 1976

The British House of Lords is the British Outer Mongolia for retired politicians.

Tony Benn, 1962

Jokers

No more coals to Newcastle, no more Hoares to Paris.
George V on the conclusion of the Hoare-Laval Pact

He let me use the [White House] pool. He only got upset when I tried to walk across the water.
Henry Kissinger, referring to Gerald Ford

There cannot be a crisis next week. My schedule is already full.
Henry Kissinger

I got a call from Haig, who offered me the job of explaining the Administration's foreign policy to the Chinese – one by one.
Henry Kissinger

I offer my opponents a bargain: if they will stop telling falsehoods about us, I will stop telling the truth about them.
attributed to both Adlai Stevenson and Senator Depew

A little nonsense now and then is not a bad thing. Where would we politicians be if we were not allowed to talk it sometimes?
Enoch Powell

Politics should be fun ...

Lord Hailsham

Is my right honourable friend saying that Wrens' skirts
must be held up until all sailors have been satisfied?
*Irene Ward MP, in the Commons after being told that
the supply of Wrens' uniforms would have to wait
until RN uniforms had been dealt with*

Do you realize the responsibility I carry? I'm the only
person standing between Nixon and the White House.

John F. Kennedy

Dead birds don't fall out of nests.

Churchill, when told his flies were undone

For God's sake don't: a joke in your mouth is no
laughing matter.
*Sheridan to Lord Lauderdale, who insisted on telling
a joke*

Cool Under Fire

I have never found in a long experience of politics that criticism is ever inhibited by ignorance.

Harold Macmillan, 1963

Cheek!
Winston Churchill, having been shot at by a sniper,
Athens, 1944

. . . a little local difficulty.
Harold Macmillan when his entire Treasury
front bench team resigned, 1959

I am grown as popular in 1821 as unpopular formerly, and, of the two, unpopularity is the more convenient and gentlemanlike.

Lord Castlereagh

Sex and Booze

But she did not say, if elected, she would not serve.
*Henry Kissinger to the Press, when Gloria Steiner
had denied a romantic link with him*

... to Westminster ... But I full of thoughts and trouble
touching the issue of this day; and to comfort myself did
go to the Dogg and drink half a pint of mulled sack, and
in the Hall did drink a dram of brandy at Mrs Howletts,
and with the warmth of this did find myself in better
order as to courage, truly. So we all up to the Lobby ...
Samuel Pepys, Diary, 5 March 1668

I've looked on a lot of women with lust. I've committed
adultery in my heart many times. God recognizes I will
do this and forgives me.

Jimmy Carter

The male sex constitutes in many ways the most
obstinate vested interest one can find.

Lord Longford

People call me the Enoch Powell of sex.

Lord Longford

Most British statesmen have either drunk too much or
womanized too much. I never fell into the second
category.

Lord George-Brown

I am notorious. I will go down in history as another Lady Hamilton.
Mandy Rice-Davies, apropos the Profumo scandal,
1963

I think any man . . . would be foolish to fool around with his secretary. If it's somebody else's secretary, fine!
Senator Barry Goldwater

Well, did you do any fornicating this weekend?
Richard M. Nixon to David Frost

No government could survive without champagne. Champagne in the throat of our diplomatic people is like oil in the wheels of an engine.
Joseph Dargent, New York Herald Tribune, 1955

Advice

The finest steel has to go through the hottest fire.
Richard M. Nixon

The best way I know of to win an argument is to start by being in the right.
Lord Hailsham

There are three groups that no British Prime Minister should provoke: the Vatican, the Treasury and the miners.
Stanley Baldwin (attrib.)

You will find in politics that you are much exposed to the attribution of false motive. Never complain and never explain.
Stanley Baldwin

. . . in the game of musical daggers: never be left holding the dagger when the music stops.
Harold Wilson

The Last Word

Go on, get out. Last words are for fools who haven't said enough.

Karl Marx

Index